CLAWS, COATS, AND CAMOUFLAGE

THE WAYS ANIMALS FIT INTO THEIR WORLD

BY SUSAN E. GOODMAN

PHOTOGRAPHS BY MICHAEL J. DOOLITTLE

THE MILLBROOK PRESS   BROOKFIELD, CONNECTICUT

To my fathers—
Irving W. Goodman
And, Sam Klein, the best father-in-law in the world.
                                                    S.E.G.

To Georgia: We had to wait a long time for you,
but you're worth every minute.   M.J.D.

All photographs by Michael Doolittle except p. 38 (middle): © Michael Fogden, Animals, Animals

Photographer's note: I would like to thank the Trevor Zoo at Millbrook School in Millbrook, New York for letting me spend time with their beautiful arctic foxes; The New England Aquarium and the Franklin Park Zoo, both in Boston, for providing invaluable information and access to their collections; and the Yacumama and Explorama Lodges in Iquitos, Peru for supporting me over the last eight years, while I explored the Amazon Rainforest and learned how to photograph in the field.

Library of Congress Cataloging-in-Publication Data
Goodman, Susan E., 1952–
Claws, coats, and camouflage : the way animals fit into their world / by Susan Goodman;
photographs by Michael Doolittle.
p. cm.
ISBN 0-7613-1865-8 (lib. bdg.)
1. Adaptation (Biology)—Juvenile literature. [1. Adaptation (Biology) 2. Animals.] I. Doolittle, Michael J. ill. II. Title.
QH546 .G66 2001
591.4—dc21   00-048167

Published by The Millbrook Press, Inc.
2 Old New Milford Road, Brookfield, Connecticut 06804
www.millbrookpress.com

CONTENTS

ADAPTATION

What would happen if you pulled a goldfish out of its bowl to play videogames? It would be in big trouble. Then again, you would be too if you went underwater without bringing any air along.

Animals live in all sorts of habitats, or environments. Some live in forests. Others live on mountains or in oceans. They have adaptations that help them fit into these worlds. Adaptations include any part of an animal's body that helps it live its special life. Adaptations also include ways an animal acts that help it survive.

Polar bears, for example, live in the freezing Arctic. They have thick fur that keeps them warm. The fur's white color lets them blend in with the snow and sneak up on animals they want to hunt. The fur is oily, so they can shake off any ice that forms after swimming.

Fur is only one of polar bears' adaptations. They also have sharp claws for grabbing their prey. Their nostrils close so they can dive underwater. They are wonderful swimmers.

The Lion's Mane sea jelly swims well too. It looks like just a beautiful pile of goo, but don't be fooled. This sea jelly has a poisonous sting that "freezes" the jelly's prey so it can't move. This is an important adaptation, because the Lion's Mane is so delicate that a thrashing fish could rip it apart.

This katydid is well adapted to living in the forest. It's hard to see, isn't it? That's a fine adaptation when birds and snakes think you're delicious.

Each animal has many adaptations. Nature gives all living things the tools they need to fit into their environment, stay safe, find food, and make babies.

FITTING IN

Animals that live in or near the water have all sorts of adaptations so they can fit into this world. They need oxygen, for example. Whales and dolphins get their oxygen by going up to the water's surface to breathe air. Fish don't.

What's this animal's adaptation?

FITTING IN: WATER

◄ **A**ll animals need oxygen to live, but not every animal uses lungs to breathe it in. Fish "breathe" with gills that take oxygen out of the water. Fish have many other adaptations for living in the water. This golden puffer fish, for example, swims by making waves with its body. It uses its fins to steer. Inside its body, it has a balloon-like organ that inflates and deflates to help it rise or dive into deeper water.

Tapirs live on land, but they always choose a home near ► water. If they spot trouble, the first thing they do is dive in. The tapir can hear, see, and breathe even when most of its body is safely underwater. That's because its ears, eyes, and nose are all located on the top part of its head.

◄ **F**lamingos have long legs, so they can stand in the water without getting their feathers all wet. Webbed feet keep them steady, even when standing in soft mud. Long necks let them stretch down into the water for a meal of brine shrimp and small clams.

Most flamingos live in and near saltwater, so they end up swallowing a lot more salt than they need. No problem—they get rid of the extra salt through glands in their nose.

FITTING IN

We can climb trees, but it would be very hard for us to spend much time up there. We don't have the right body for it.

What's this animal's adaptation?

FITTING IN: FOREST

◄ **T**he orangutan's long arms and strong hands are perfect for living in the tropical rain forest. Walking, climbing, and swinging from branch to branch, orangutans spend almost all their time in the treetops. They even sleep up there. At night, they build a platform-like nest out of branches that they use as a bed.

Tree frogs are great climbers too, but they have different equipment. All their toes have round pads that grip onto things. The pads also produce a sticky goo that helps tree frogs climb the smoothest branch. ►

◄ **T**oo slow to run from predators, the chameleon hides by changing color and blending in. Its body is perfectly shaped for life on a tree limb. Its flat sides keep its weight squarely centered on the branch. Its feet grip the branches firmly, three toes clamping down on one side and two on the other. Having a tail that works like a lasso doesn't hurt either.

FITTING IN

The llama lives high in the Andes Mountains, where it is always cool and often freezing.

What's this animal's adaptation?

FITTING IN: COLD

◄ **T**he llama's coat is very long and thick. Just as important, each hair has tiny air pockets inside of it. This trapped air keeps the cold from getting through to the llama's skin.

The arctic fox has a warm winter coat too—living near ► the North Pole, it needs it. Thick fur covers its ears, even the soles of its feet. The arctic fox thinks 40 degrees below zero Fahrenheit (-40 degrees Celsius) is just another fine winter day. If the day gets colder, it just curls up and covers its nose with its tail.

The arctic fox's white fur makes it hard ► to see against the ice and snow of winter. When summer comes, however, the fox sheds its winter coat and grows a grayish-brown one that matches the dirt and rocks.

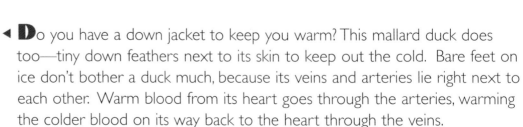

◄ **D**o you have a down jacket to keep you warm? This mallard duck does too—tiny down feathers next to its skin to keep out the cold. Bare feet on ice don't bother a duck much, because its veins and arteries lie right next to each other. Warm blood from its heart goes through the arteries, warming the colder blood on its way back to the heart through the veins.

FITTING IN

Camels live in the desert where it is hard to survive.

What's this animal's adaptation❓

FITTING IN: HEAT

 ◄ **C**amels don't store water in their humps as many people think. But they can go days, even weeks, without drinking by saving the water stored in their bodies. They can change their body temperature up to 11 degrees Fahrenheit (6 degrees Celsius) to keep from sweating. In groups, they press against each other to keep cooler. And, when they do find water, they tank up. Camels can drink 25 gallons (95 liters) of water in just ten minutes.

◄ **T**his tortoise lives in the desert too. Unless it rains, the tortoise doesn't find much to drink. So it gets most of its water from the plants it eats. Its body also removes the waste products from its urine and uses the watery part again.

Desert animals aren't the only ones that deal with heat. ► People keep their bodies cool by sweating. Dogs sweat too, but just a little bit. Dogs can sweat only through their feet. The main way they get rid of heat is to pant, to breathe it out.

FITTING IN

This monkey is nocturnal. It rests during the day and is active at night. It needs special equipment to live this dark, nighttime life.

What's this animal's adaptation?

FITTING IN: NIGHT

▲ This night monkey has large eyes. In fact, they're huge. If your eyes were as big, they would take up most of your face. These eyes let the night monkey take in what little light there is at night so it can see.

▲ When hunting at night, this leaf-nosed bat doesn't rely on its eyes to find its insect dinner. Instead, it "sees" perfectly with its ears. It sends out sounds that bump up against things and bounce back in its direction. Using echoes from tree trunks, branches, and, of course, delicious insects, the bat creates a clear picture of its world.

◀ In the black of night, some of the best animal hunters miss their prey. Not the Sumatran pit viper. This snake has a special organ on its face that senses heat. It tells the snake when the warm body of a small animal is nearby. Then the pit viper closes in and strikes with its venom-filled fangs.

Staying Safe

You can't eat what you can't see. One way animals stay safe is to stay hidden.

What's this animal's adaptation ?

STAYING SAFE: CAMOUFLAGE

◄ **T**his gecko might win its game of hide-and-seek with a predator. It is well camouflaged because it is sitting on a plant-coated tree trunk that matches its coloring. To stay hidden, camouflaged animals must also remain perfectly still.

Shape can help an animal blend in too. This ► plant is a perfect hiding place for a grasshopper with a twiggy shape and light coloring.

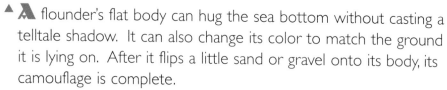

▲ **A** flounder's flat body can hug the sea bottom without casting a telltale shadow. It can also change its color to match the ground it is lying on. After it flips a little sand or gravel onto its body, its camouflage is complete.

STAYING SAFE

Camouflage is only one way animals fool their predators.

What's this animal's adaptation **?**

STAYING SAFE:
BLUFFS AND DISGUISES

This owl butterfly has a trick to fool predators. The spots ▶ on its wings look like the eyes of a bigger creature. A hungry bird might be scared off by these eye-spots without ever really seeing the tasty butterfly. Or it might attack the "eyes" and end up with a beakful of wing instead of a real meal.

◀ The golden butterfly fish takes this trick one step further. A black stripe covers each of its real eyes. Then the back of its body is shaped so the gap below its eyespot looks like a big mouth.

Did you have a hard time picking the katydid out from the ▶ leaves? That's what this insect is counting on. The katydid looks like a dead leaf in order to hide from its enemies. Some dead leaf katydids even have "moldy spots" and "chewed-up" edges to complete their disguises. Other insects that use disguises look like thorns, sticks, even bird droppings!

STAYING SAFE

Some animals don't try to hide. They aren't interested in fooling predators at all.

What's this animal's adaptation

STAYING SAFE: WARNING COLORS

◄ **S**ome animals smell bad or taste bad or are poisonous. Their bright colors and patterns are like a sign that says, "Stay away from me—I'm trouble."

If a predator bites this poison-arrow frog, it might be killed by the frog's poisonous skin. If the predator does survive, it knows not to try again.

The lionfish isn't brightly colored, but it's ► easy to spot. A good thing—you wouldn't want to touch one by accident. The lionfish uses its poisonous spines to defend itself. It hunts by driving little fish into a corner with its frilly fins. Then it uses its mouth like a vacuum to suck in its prey.

◄ **S**kunks use warning colors, just not colorful ones. A thick white stripe is very noticeable at night when skunks are active. If something bothers a skunk, it doesn't hide. Instead, it raises its white tail to remind the enemy that there's a stinky price to pay for coming closer.

STAYING SAFE

Some animals can't protect themselves by fighting well or running fast.

What's this animal's adaptation ❓

STAYING SAFE: HARD TO EAT

The horseshoe crab doesn't have a lot of predators. Who'd want to ▶ bother? The horseshoe crab looks more like a tank than a meal. Armored with such a hard shell, it is very hard to eat.

◀ **P**orcupines aren't such an easy mouthful either— not with 30,000 quills on their backs and tails. When threatened, the porcupine turns around and raises its quills. If it backs into an enemy, dozens of quills go into the attacker's skin—and stay there. Bobcats and coyotes have starved to death because their mouths were so full of quills that they couldn't eat.

◀ **T**he clownfish doesn't have a hard shell or quills, but it's still hard to eat. The clownfish makes its home in a stinging anemone. It isn't bothered by the anemone's sting, but other creatures are. Once a predator chases the clownfish and gets zapped by the anemone, it learns to stay away.

STAYING SAFE

Animals that live alone can depend only
upon themselves for defense.

What are these animals' adaptations?

STAYING SAFE: SAFETY IN NUMBERS

◄ **M**any fish, like these herring, band together in groups called schools. Predators can get confused seeing so many fish together. They may have a hard time picking out and chasing an individual fish. Sometimes small fish in schools swim so close together that predators think they are one big creature.

Puffins gather and have their babies ► on small islands to stay away from hungry mammals. But the black-backed seagull is still a problem. So puffins often fly in wide circles over their nesting grounds. Birds leaving the colony join the circle and then break off when they fly out to sea. Returning birds join the circle and drop out near their own nests. These "puffin wheels" lessen the chance that any one puffin will be singled out and killed.

◄ **P**aper wasps live in colonies too. Every wasp has a job to do, working for the good of the nest. The queen lays eggs. Some workers get food. Others feed and tend the babies. Still others guard the nest against predators. Even if many workers die, chances are that enough will survive for the nest to go on.

GETTING FOOD

Animals need good equipment if they are going to catch other animals to eat.

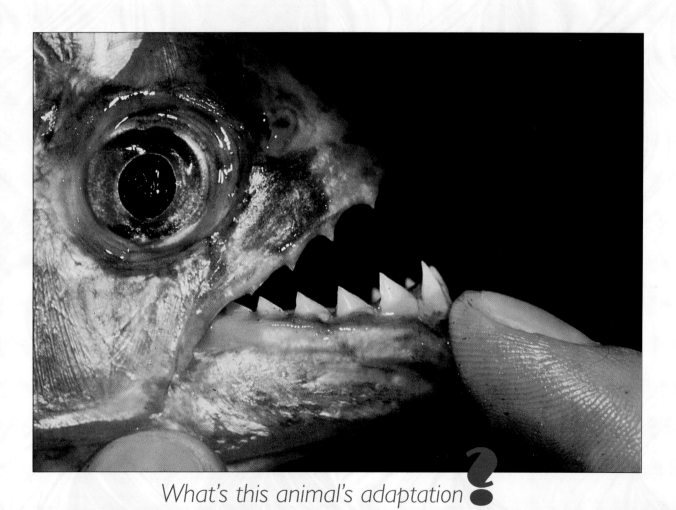

What's this animal's adaptation?

GETTING FOOD: GREAT HUNTING TOOLS

◄ **P**iranha may be small, but their razor-sharp teeth do a lot of damage. Piranha travel in groups and usually prey on other fish. But they can also reduce a larger (usually wounded) animal to a skeleton in no time at all.

◄ **T**eeth are good hunting tools; so are claws. A lobster's claws are almost as long as its body. One claw is big with thick edges to crush prey. The smaller one has sharper edges to tear things apart. Whether the lobster is hiding in its burrow during the day or prowling the ocean bottom at night, its claws are ready to grab any meal that comes its way.

◄ **B**e glad you're big because a red-tailed hawk is a dangerous killing machine. Its eyes, ten times better than yours, can spot prey far, far away. Its strong claws, or talons, are perfect for grabbing a victim off the ground or plucking it from midair. Its sharp, hooked beak can finish the job by tearing off strips of flesh.

GETTING FOOD

Plant-eating animals need the right kinds of tools too.

What's this animal's adaptation **?**

GETTING FOOD:
PLANT-EATING TOOLS

◄ **N**ectar is sometimes located deep inside a flower. Butterflies have a way to get at it. They have a proboscis, a tube that comes out from their mouth. When they find a flower, they uncoil their proboscis and push it in. They use it like a straw to suck up the nectar.

▲ **W**arthogs like eating grass but also underground roots and bulbs. Their spadelike snouts help them dig in the dirt for those treats. So do their tusks, which are actually extra big teeth. The warthogs' eyes are set very high on their heads. That's so they can dig and eat, while keeping an eye out for danger.

◄ **L**eaf-cutter ants live in huge groups of a million or more. To feed their colony, worker ants snip bits of leaves with their scissor-like jaws and bring the scraps home. But leaf-cutter ants don't eat the leaves. These

ants are farmers that use the leaves to grow their food. Inside the colony, small worker ants chew the leaves to mix them with saliva. This spongy gunk is the perfect place to grow the fungus that the ants like to eat.

GETTING FOOD

Animals hunted as food aren't the only ones who need to hide.

What's this animal's adaptation?

GETTING FOOD: CAMOUFLAGE

◄ **A**nimals that hunt also rely on camouflage. They need to hide from their prey. This spotted scorpionfish waits on ledges or the ocean floor. To passing fish, it is just another rock—until it's too late.

▲ **F**lowers are pretty things, but they can be pretty dangerous too. Insects that go to certain flowers looking for nectar may find this goldenrod spider instead. Blending in, it stays perfectly still. It grabs its prey with its front legs and uses venom to stop it from moving. Then it sucks the insect dry.

The goldenrod spider uses white flowers as its hunting ground. And yellow ones. It changes its color to match.

◄ **T**he snow leopard doesn't just sit around waiting for a wild sheep or gazelle to come its way. It stalks its prey, following it, watching it. Its smoke-colored fur with blurry gray spots makes it blend right in with the surrounding rocks and boulders until the moment is right to strike.

GETTING FOOD

Some animals chase after their prey.
Others do not.

What's this animal's adaptation

GETTING FOOD: LETTING FOOD COME TO YOU

◄ This golden orb-weaver spider can capture a meal without moving very far. It spins a web and waits. When an insect gets caught in the sticky threads, it feels its vibrations and rushes over. It does not get stuck itself because it has oil on its body. It wraps up its prey and eats it whenever it's ready.

▲ The basket star's arms are like a spider's web. Small bits of food get tangled in its branching arms as they float by. That's why this animal chooses to live in parts of the ocean with a strong current.

▲ This tree lizard knows all the best places to feast on bees. Green like the surrounding leaves, it waits, perfectly still, near a bunch of flowers. When the bees buzz over to dine on nectar, they become dinner instead.

GETTING FOOD

Some animals like finding food that can't run away.

What's this animal's adaptation ?

GETTING FOOD: LETTING SOMEONE ELSE DO THE WORK

◄ **S**ea gulls do eat live fish and insects. But they are also great scavengers. That means they eat nonliving things—dead animals and food scraps—that they find on the ground or in the water. Some people think sea gulls are pests. Yet these birds help keep beaches clean by feeding on garbage left by messy humans.

Coyotes and ► ravens also eat just about anything they can find, including dead animals and garbage. Here, they are guarding what's left of an elk. Scavengers remove dead animals from the environment before they become infected and threaten living ones with disease.

◄ **U**nlike these other scavengers, vultures eat *only* dead animals. They have many adaptations that help them survive on this kind of diet. Their excellent sense of smell helps them find rotting meat. Their strong beaks tear through tough hides. Not having feathers on their heads and necks also makes good sense. Vultures, like this King vulture, don't get their heads all dirty when they dip into a rotten carcass.

MAKING A NEW GENERATION

When most animals get together to mate, the males try to attract the females. Then the females do the choosing. It's no different for turkeys.

What's this animal's adaptation

MAKING A NEW GENERATION: ATTRACTING A MATE

▲ **J**ust like a male peacock spreading his tail, this male turkey is showing off. During mating season, the colors on his head and throat get brighter. He fans his tail feathers and makes loud gobbling sounds. The colors and the sounds are like a television commercial for female turkeys. It says, "I'm healthy. I'm strong. Pick me."

Male elk don't wait around for females ▶ to decide. They fight over them instead. If one bull can't scare the other off, they lock antlers and start pushing. The biggest, strongest bulls usually win the fight and get to mate with the females.

The male satin bowerbird has ▶ another way to attract females—home decorating. He uses sticks to build a bower, or stage, to dance on with his mate. Then he decorates it—using as many blue things as possible to match his feathers. He paints its walls with the blue juice of berries. He arranges bright objects like flowers, beetles, and shells. Then he waits.

This system helps make sure that the strongest, healthiest elk are parenting the new generation.

MAKING A NEW GENERATION

Some animals take care of themselves from birth. Some fish, turtles, and insects never even see their parents. Other newborns need help from mom or dad.

What's this animal's adaptation **?**

MAKING A NEW GENERATION: KEEPING THEM SAFE

◄ **N**ewborn emperor scorpions are totally helpless. They are unable to sting or eat. Sometimes their mother will dig a nest for them in a termite mound. Most of the time, they ride on her back. In about a week, they are ready to live on their own.

Kittens are blind ► at birth and need their mother's protection. Mother cats stay close and guard their young. They can carry a kitten by gently biting down on a loose flap of skin on the back of the kitten's neck.

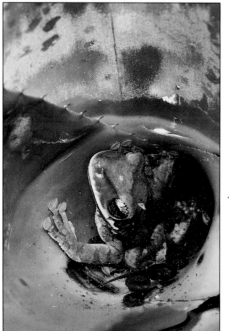

◄ **B**irds have nests. Foxes have dens. And this mother tree frog has her bromeliad tank, attached to a rain-forest tree. A bromeliad plant has leaves that circle around each other and form a little tank. Rain fills the tank and makes it a perfect place for a tree frog to lay her eggs. They hatch into tadpoles, which eat the bugs that fall into their watery home.

MAKING A NEW GENERATION

Babies are born hungry and have to be fed.

What's this animal's adaptation?

MAKING A NEW GENERATION: FEEDING THEM

◄ **T**his macaque monkey is a mammal. Mammal mothers don't worry about finding the right foods for their new babies. They can feed the babies milk made right in their own bodies. A lot of animals are mammals, including horses and elephants, pigs and dogs.

▲ **R**obins have to hunt for their babies' food. Mothers, and sometimes fathers, go out to find earthworms, grasshoppers, beetle grubs, and berries. Feeding three to five hungry babies is a full-time job. A baby robin can eat 14 feet (4 meters) of worms in one day.

◄ **T**he queen of this bullet ant colony does not feed her babies. She's too busy laying eggs. So her grown-up daughters take the job. The oldest, largest worker ants go out and find food like this grasshopper. Smaller workers feed it, piece by piece, to the ant larvae.

HUMAN BEINGS ARE ANIMALS TOO.

What's this animal's adaptation❗

FITTING IN

STAYING SAFE

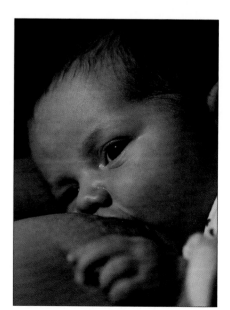

MAKING A NEW GENERATION

GETTING FOOD

FEEDING A NEW GENERATION

HAVING A
LANGUAGE

LIVING IN A
COMMUNITY

INDEX